BALD KNOBBER

BY ROBERT SERGEL

BALD KNOBBER
FIRST EDITION © 2018

PRINTED IN CHINA

ISBN-13: 978-0-9991935-1-8
ISBN-10: 0-9991935-1-1

LIBRARY OF CONGRESS PCN: 2017958130

PUBLISHED BY SECRET ACRES
200 PARK AVENUE SOUTH, 8TH FLOOR
NEW YORK, NY 10003

SA040

THANK YOU BARRY, LEON, EVE, MY FRIENDS + FAMILY
SPECIAL THANKS TO JEREMY (RIP) WHO WAS ON MY
MIND A LOT WHILE I MADE THIS THING.

ONE

THE BEST PART IS PROBABLY WHEN THEY PUSH THE FAT KID OFF A CLIFF.

SUMMER

EITHER THAT OR THE TALKING PIG SKULL.

GLAD YOU ENJOYED IT, SAM. HAVE A SEAT.

WHY DON'T WE HEAR FROM COLE NEXT?

MY REPORT IS ON A BOOK CALLED...

BALD KNOBBERS
VIGILANTES OF THE OZARKS

IT'S A TRUE STORY ABOUT MISSOURI IN THE 1880S.
HAPPY BIRTHDAY, KIDDO.
HONK
HONK
HONK

THE CIVIL WAR HAD ENDED...
YOUR MOM IS HERE.

...BUT THINGS WERE STILL REALLY BAD.

TELL THAT MANTIS HER CHECK IS IN THE MAIL.

MISSOURI HAD BEEN SHARPLY DIVIDED DURING THE WAR.

THERE WAS STILL A LOT OF BAD BLOOD...
GROW UP, ASSHOLE.

...WHICH MADE THE LAW DIFFICULT TO ENFORCE.
SMASH!

MARAUDING BUSHWHACKERS TOOK FULL ADVANTAGE OF THE SITUATION.

THEY'D ATTACK VULNERABLE FAMILIES AND DESTROY THEIR HOMES.

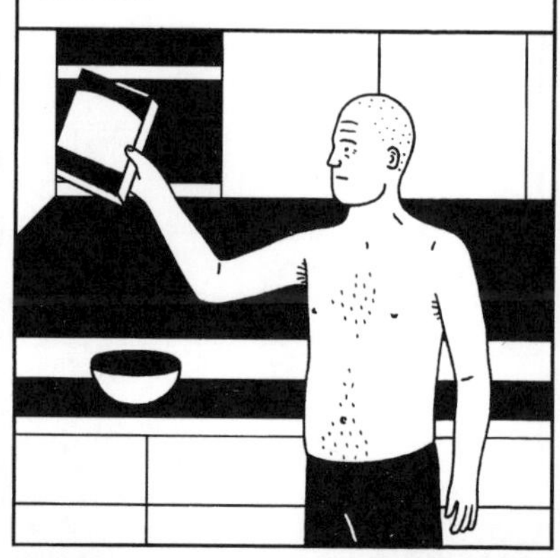

IT WAS TOTAL ANARCHY.

AUTHORITIES WERE BIASED AND UNRELIABLE.
YOU'RE NOT BEING FAIR, COLE.

BRAD IS A REALLY NICE GUY! JUST GIVE HIM A CHANCE!

THEY COULDN'T BE TRUSTED.
WHERE ARE YOU GOING?

I'M TAKING DAISY FOR A WALK.

ONE DAY A SMALL GROUP MET ON A HILLTOP.

THEY AGREED THAT THINGS WERE OUT OF CONTROL...

...SO THEY CAME UP WITH A SECRET PLAN.

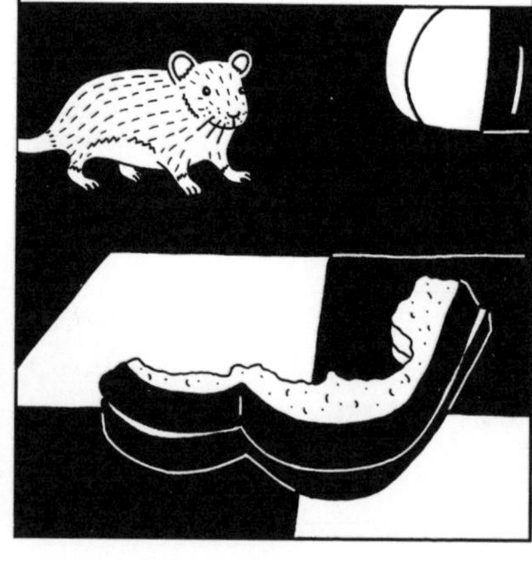
THEY WOULD RESTORE ORDER IN MISSOURI...

...BY ANY MEANS NECESSARY.

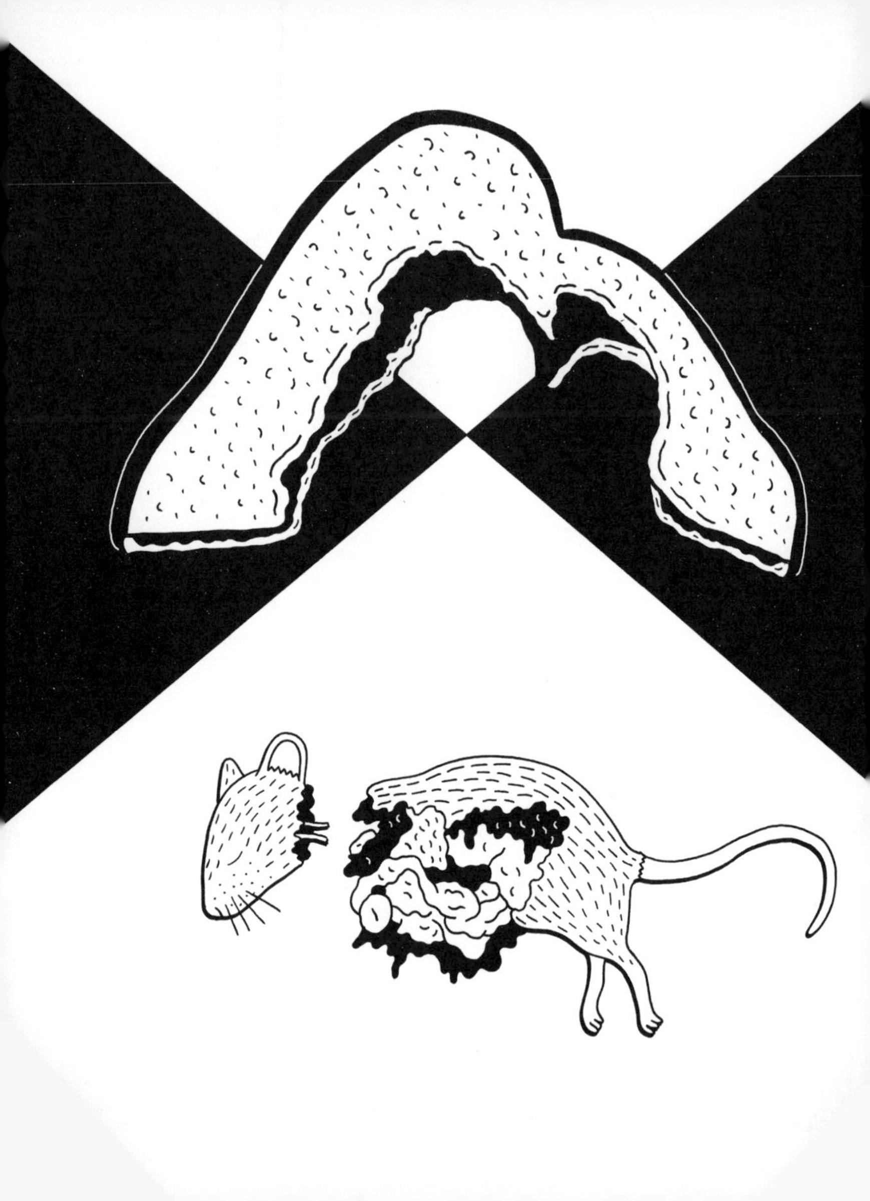

TWO

THEY CALLED THEMSELVES THE BALD KNOBBERS AFTER A TREELESS HILL WHERE THEY MET.
EVOLU

THEY WORE COOL MASKS WITH HORNS ON THEM...

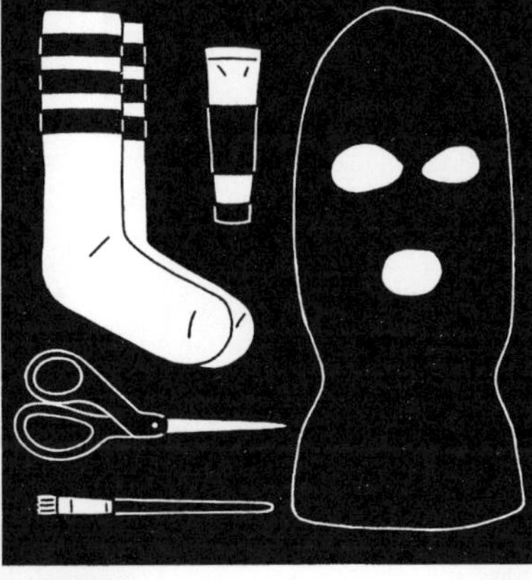

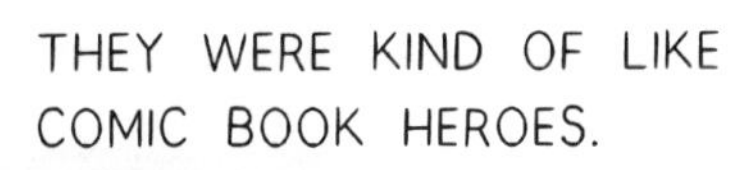

THE MASKS HID THEIR TRUE IDENTITIES...

BUT THEY ALSO LOOKED REALLY SCARY...

...TO STRIKE FEAR IN THE HEARTS OF THEIR ENEMIES.

KNOBBER ATTACK!!!

DAD?
ZZZZZ

SOMETIMES THE REAL WORLD IS LIKE A COMIC BOOK.
OH LOOK IT'S JANKY BATMAN.

THERE ARE GOOD GUYS...
I'M A BALD KNOBBER.

...AND THERE ARE BAD GUYS.
HA! NO GRASS ON THE FIELD, HUH?

YOU CAN'T REASON
WITH BAD GUYS.
HOW'S YOUR
MOM, COLE?

I HEARD SHE'S
FUCKING SOME
GREASE MONKEY.

I BET HER PUSSY SMELLS
LIKE MOTOR OIL.

THEY ONLY UNDERSTAND
ONE THING.
TSSSSS

YOU HAVE TO BE BAD RIGHT BACK.
SLAP
!

I KNOW THEY SAY THAT VIOLENCE IS NEVER THE ANSWER...

...AND THAT TWO WRONGS DON'T MAKE A RIGHT.

I DON'T DISAGREE WITH ANY OF THAT STUFF...

...BUT THERE'S DEFINITELY SOME GREY AREA.

SO THE NEXT TIME AN INJUSTICE WAS COMMITTED...

...THE BALD KNOBBERS SPRANG INTO ACTION.

THEY TRACKED DOWN
THE BAD GUYS...

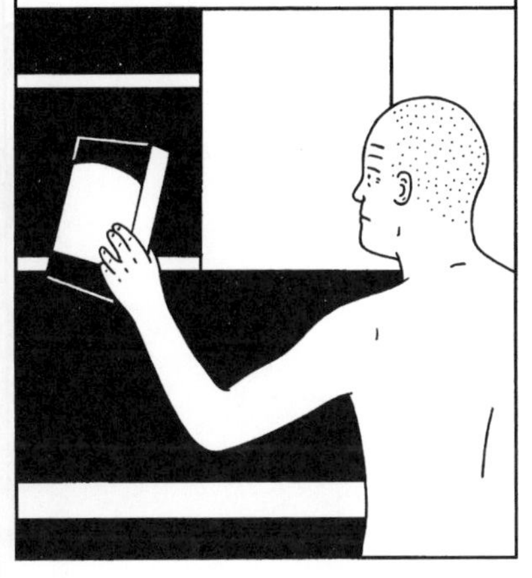

TIED ROPES AROUND
THEIR NECKS...

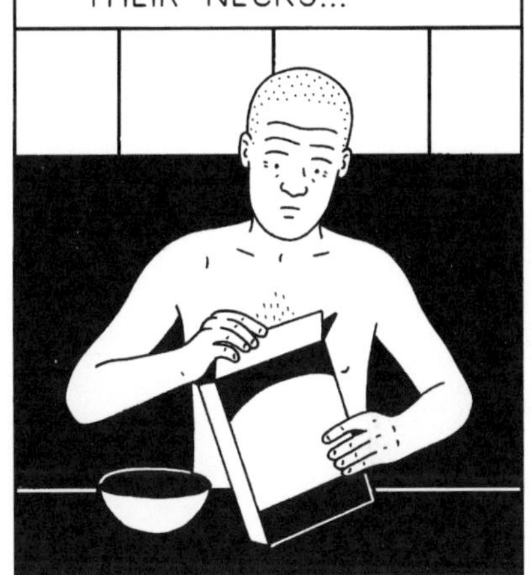

...AND LET GRAVITY
DO THE REST.

THEN THEY STUCK
A WARNING NOTE TO
ONE OF THE BODIES.

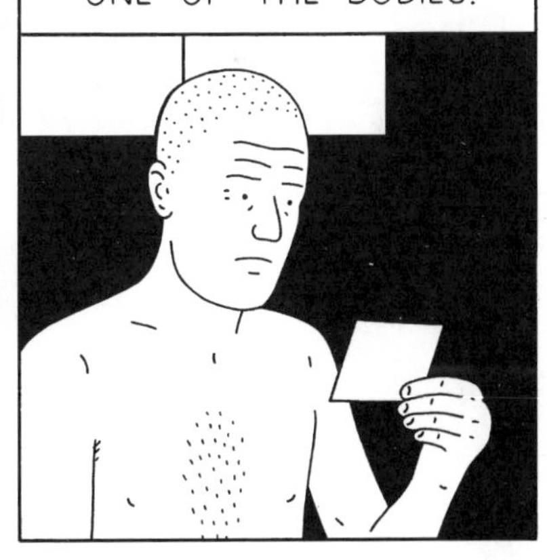

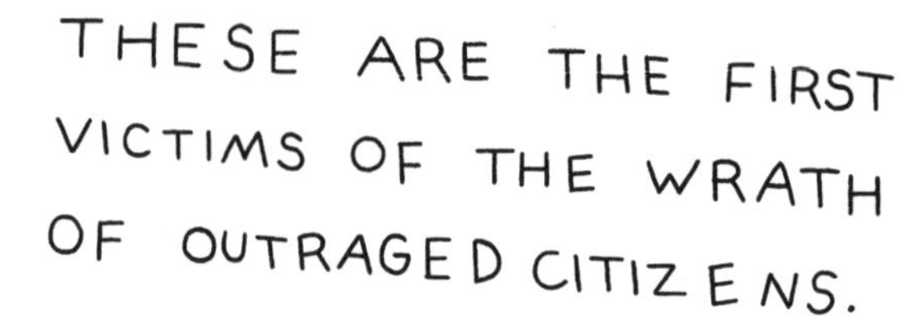
THESE ARE THE FIRST VICTIMS OF THE WRATH OF OUTRAGED CITIZENS.
MORE WILL FOLLOW.
-THE BALD KNOBBERS

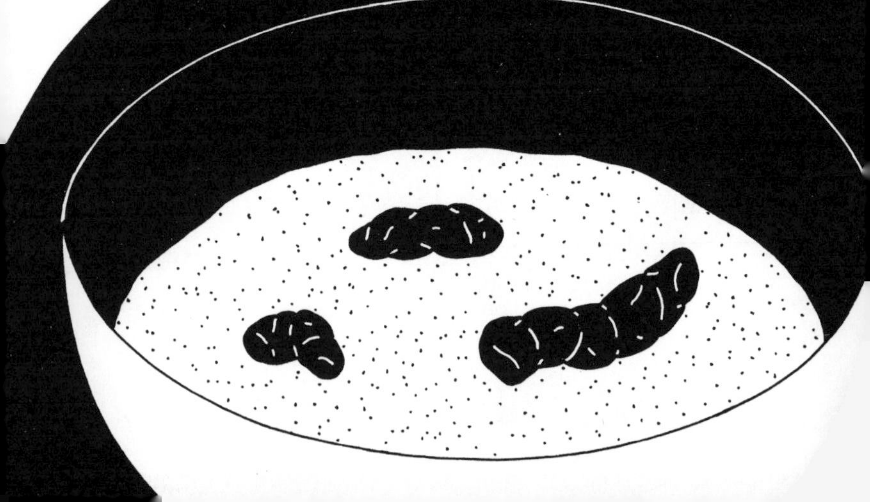

THREE

NEWS OF THE KNOBBERS SPREAD QUICKLY ACROSS THE COUNTY.
SUMM
RE DI

NOT EVERYONE APPROVED OF THEIR TACTICS.
COLE! GET YOUR BUTT OUT HERE!

TAKE OFF THAT STUPID MASK AND GET IN THE CAR!

WE ARE DRIVING TO BRAD'S GARAGE, AND YOU ARE GOING TO APOLOGIZE!

FRONTIER JUSTICE HAD RUFFLED SOME FEATHERS.
I DID NOT RAISE A SOCIOPATH...

THE AUTHORITIES WERE RIGHTLY CONCERNED.
BE NICE! I'LL SEE YOU AFTER WORK.

IT WAS ONLY A MATTER OF TIME...
AUTO REPAIR

...BEFORE THEY GOT WHAT WAS COMING TO THEM.
HEY COLE...

YOU GONNA PEE IN MY GAS TANK OR SOMETHING?

I'M SORRY ABOUT THE CEREAL THING. IT WAS STUPID.

DON'T WORRY ABOUT IT.

I GUESS IT WAS KINDA FUNNY....
BRAD

...IN A DAHMER SORT OF WAY.

ANYWAY...I GET THAT YOU DON'T LIKE ME VERY MUCH.

AND I KNOW THERE'S NOTHING I CAN SAY TO CHANGE YOUR MIND...
UNZIP

...SO I'LL SPARE YOU A SPEECH ABOUT WHAT A "GOOD GUY" I AM.

HAHA...RELAX. IT'S A BB GUN.

PEPSI

TEN BUCKS SAYS YOU DON'T MAKE A DENT.

PEPSI
POP!

FORK IT OVER, GAS MAN.

JUSTICE SWEPT ACROSS THE LAND LIKE A WAVE.

CORRUPT OFFICIALS WERE BRANDED LIKE CATTLE. THIEVES WERE BEATEN BLOODY OR HANGED.

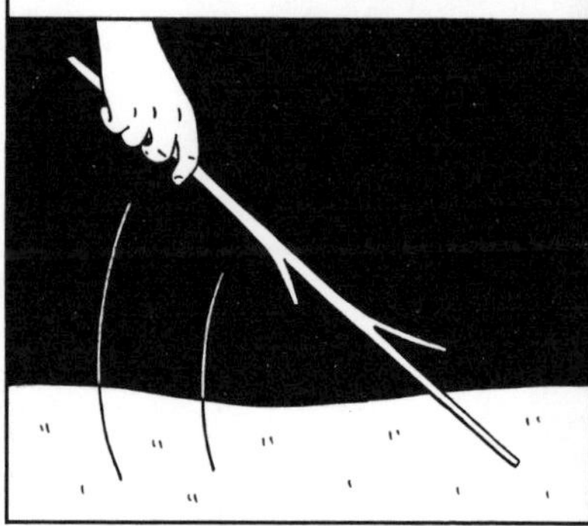

DRUNKARDS AND LOOSE WOMEN WERE WHIPPED WITHOUT MERCY.

IT WAS ALL GOING LIKE THEY PLANNED UNTIL...

WE DON'T CALL WOMEN "LOOSE" IN THIS CLASSROOM.

BUT THAT'S HOW THEY SAY IT IN THE BOOK...

IT'S NOT APPROPRIATE. DROP IT.

SORRY...WHERE WAS I?

I LOST MY PLACE.

FOUR

OH YEAH...
THEN SOMEONE
BURNED DOWN THE
COURTHOUSE.

NO ONE KNEW WHO DID IT...

...BUT EVERYONE BLAMED THE BALD KNOBBERS.

YOU DIDN'T HAVE ANYTHING TO...DO WITH THIS, RIGHT?

IT JUST SEEMED LIKE SOMETHING THEY'D DO.

THE FIRE WAS A HUGE NEWS STORY...
COULD IT BE ARSON?
7

...SO THE MISSOURI GOVERNOR DEMANDED AN INVESTIGATION.
I WOULDN'T RULE ANYTHING OUT AT THIS POINT.

I'LL LET YOU KNOW WHAT WE FIND...
FIRE MARSHAL

...OR IF THE CAT TURNS UP.

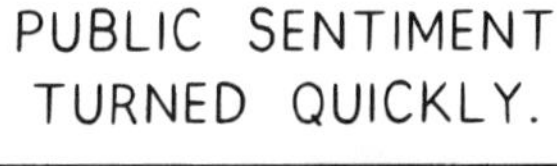
PUBLIC SENTIMENT TURNED QUICKLY.

CAN'T WE TRY CALLING DAD AGAIN?
IT'S LATE, SWEETIE.

OPPONENTS FORMED A GROUP OF THEIR OWN.

THEY WERE CALLED THE ANTI-BALD KNOBBERS.
I NEED TO LIE DOWN.

THE COUCH IS PRETTY COMFORTABLE. I SLEEP ON IT ALL THE TIME.

IT WAS AN UNHOLY ALLIANCE.

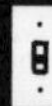

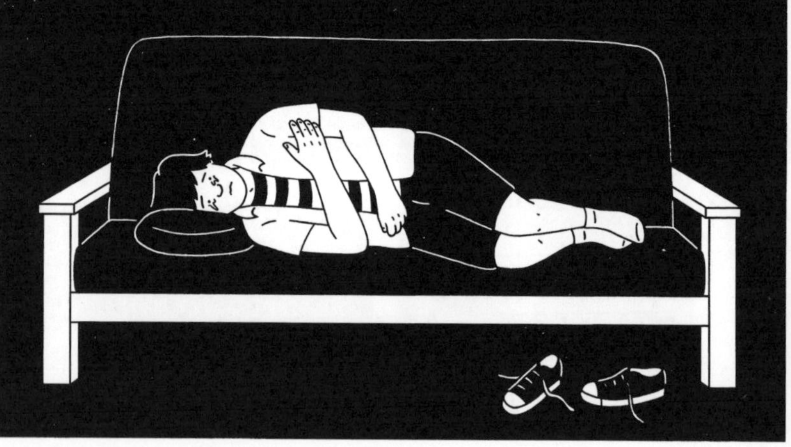

THE CORRUPT LOCAL OFFICIALS...

JOINED FORCES WITH KNOWN CRIMINALS...

...TO WIPE OUT THE KNOBBERS FOR GOOD.
12
9
3
6

THEY EVEN SANG A SONG ABOUT IT...

THESE KNOBBERS RUN THE COUNTRY...

DAISY...
RUSTLE
RUSTLE

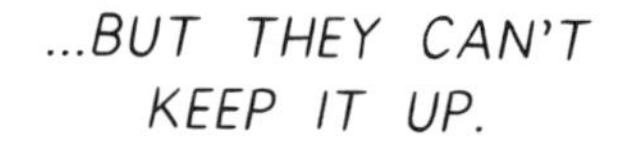
...BUT THEY CAN'T KEEP IT UP.

Nubbin
Hill
BAR &
GRILL

THEY'LL STICK THEIR TAIL BETWEEN THEIR LEGS...
HONK
HONK

...LIKE ANY OTHER PUP.
ARE YOU GOING TO TELL MOM?

JUST GET IN... SHE'S GOT ENOUGH TO WORRY ABOUT.

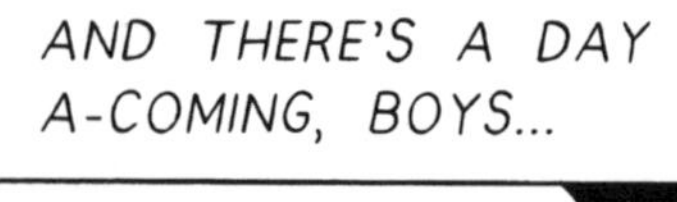
AND THERE'S A DAY A-COMING, BOYS...

STILL NO ANSWER! UNBELIEVABLE!

IF WE'RE LUCKY HE'S DEAD IN A GUTTER SOMEWHERE...

SORRY...I DIDN'T MEAN THAT. I'M JUST FRUSTRATED.

...WHEN THEY WILL HUNT THEIR DENS.
I THINK YOU BOTH BELONG IN A GUTTER.

AND IF I'M NOT MISTAKEN...
TOWN

Nubbin Hill BAR & GRILL
OPEN

...THERE SOME WILL FIND THEIR ENDS.

FIVE

THE SITUATION ONLY GOT WORSE FROM THERE.

AS THE CASUALTIES CONTINUED TO MOUNT...

DAD?

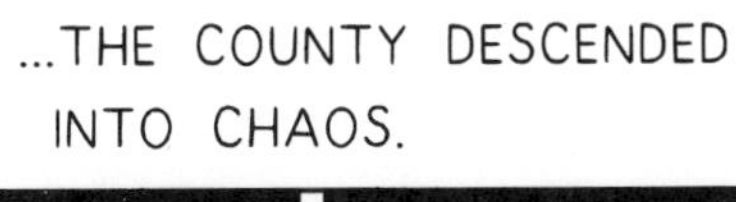

THE BAD BLOOD TURNED EVERYONE INTO ANIMALS.
I SCRREWD UPPKIDDO...

ORDER COULD NOT BE RESTORED.
IT'S ALLL OVERR...

ANY HOPE THAT STILL REMAINED...
SMASH
BUS

...WAS SHATTERED INTO A MILLION LITTLE PIECES.

THE KNOBBERS HAD TRIED TO HELP...

...BUT THEY'D ONLY MADE THINGS WORSE.

AND UNFORTUNATELY FOR THEM...

...THE WORST WAS YET TO COME.

I GUESS THAT'S THE THING WITH VIOLENCE.

IT SEEMS LIKE A GOOD IDEA AT THE TIME...
SHOVE!

...BUT IT USUALLY COMES BACK TO GET YOU IN THE END.
PUNCH

YOU CAN'T REALLY ESCAPE IT.
STOP SQUIRMING, FAGGOT!

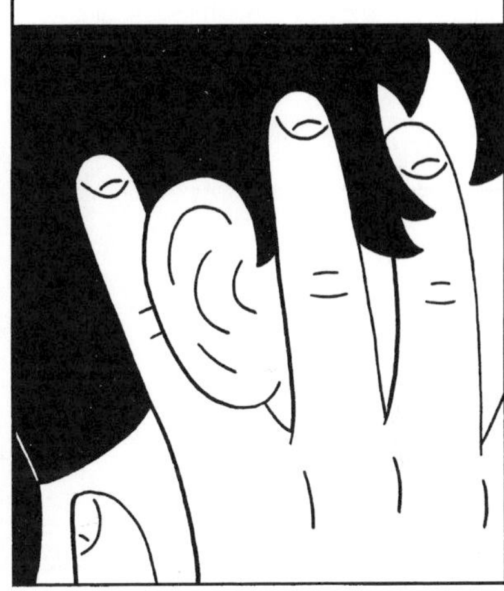
IT'S A CYCLE.

IT WILL CHEW YOU UP...

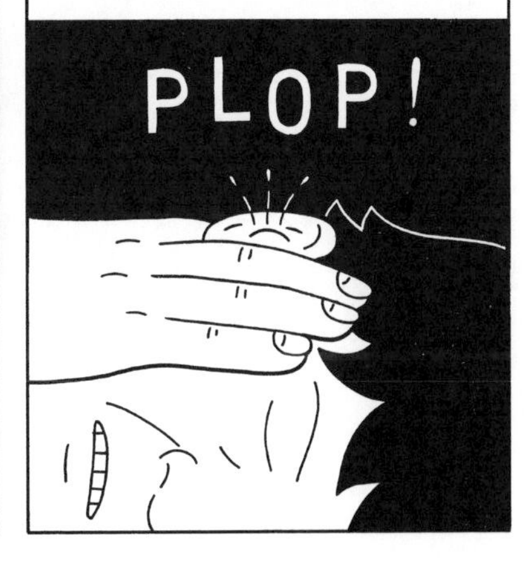
...AND SPIT YOU BACK OUT AGAIN.
PLOP!

THE BEGINNING OF THE END WAS ONE NIGHT AFTER A MEETING...

SOME ANGRY BALD KNOBBERS BROKE IN-TO A FARM HOUSE...
YANK!

...AND KILLED THE FAMILY INSIDE.

THEY HADN'T DONE ANYTHING WRONG. IT WAS SENSELESS.

THE MURDERS SPARKED NATIONAL OUTRAGE...

...AND THE KNOBBERS WERE DECLARED A PUBLIC MENACE.

THUNK!

THEY'D HAVE TO ANSWER FOR THEIR CRIMES.

KNOCK
KNOCK

FIRE
MARSHAL

SIX

THE KILLERS WERE TRIED AND SENTENCED TO DEATH.

AT THE INSISTENCE OF THE GOVERNOR...
Nubbin Hill BAR & GRILL

I APPRECIATE THE DETECTIVE WORK, KID...

...BUT WE'RE CERTAIN IT WAS BAD WIRING.

...THE BALD KNOBBERS AGREED TO DISBAND.
GLAD TO SEE THE CAT TURNED UP, THOUGH.

A TRUCE WAS DECLARED.

BUT THE LEADER OF THE KNOBBERS...

I'M SORRY ABOUT EARLIER, SWEETIE.

...HAD MADE TOO MANY ENEMIES.

THE ANTI-BALD KNOBBERS HELD ONE FINAL MEETING...

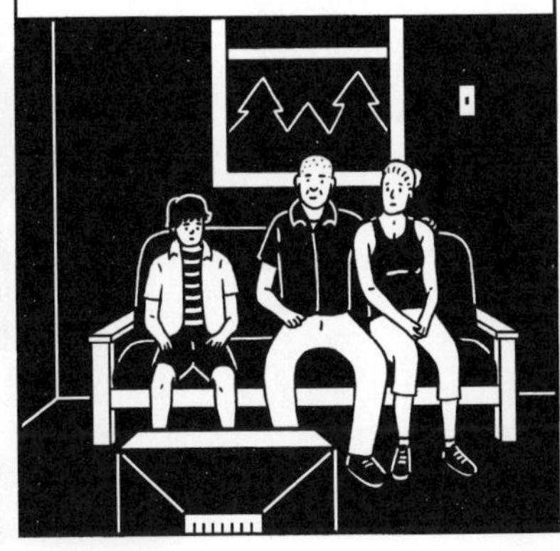

...AND AN ASSASSIN WAS CHOSEN.

WHEN HE WASN'T EXPECTING IT...

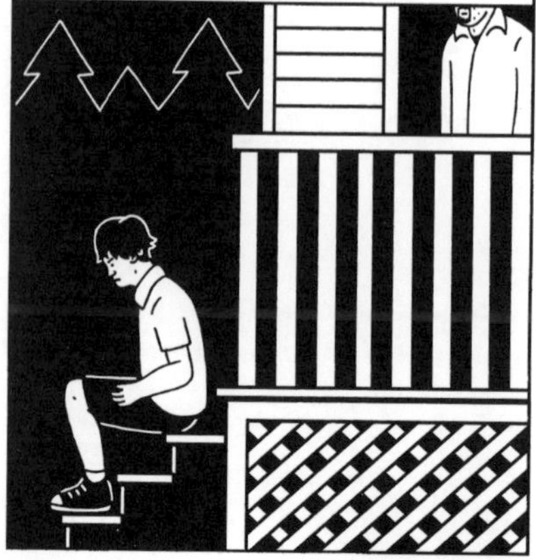

THE KNOBBER CHIEF WAS AMBUSHED...

...AND SHOT RIGHT IN THE HEART.

YOU HAVE EVERY RIGHT TO BE MAD.

I'M SO ASHAMED THAT YOU SAW ME LIKE THAT...

...AND THAT I WASN'T THERE FOR YOU GUYS WHEN YOU NEEDED ME.

I THINK MAYBE THE SPLIT HIT ME HARD AND IT JUST KINDA GOT OUT OF HAND.

BUT I DON'T WANT TO MAKE EXCUSES, AND I DON'T EXPECT YOU TO FORGIVE ME ANYTIME SOON.

THAT'S PRETTY MUCH WHERE IT ENDS.

THE BOOK IS KIND OF BORING AFTER THAT.

THE COURT HOUSE WAS REBUILT.

LIFE IN THE COUNTY WASN'T PERFECT...
COLE! YOU'RE GONNA BE LATE FOR SCHOOL!

BUT EVERYONE TRIED TO BE MORE CIVIL...
hosen
assassin
and shot him
That's pretty much
ok is kind of boring
t house was rebuilt. Life
but everyone trie

...BECAUSE THEY HAD TO BE.
BE RIGHT DOWN!

THEY'D SEEN WHAT IT WAS LIKE...

WHEN VIGILANTES RULE THE LAND...

...AND IT WAS A TOTAL NIGHTMARE.
KINNEY MIDDLE SCHOOL

THAT'S IT.

WELL DONE! THAT SOUNDS LIKE A VERY INTERESTING BOOK.

MINDY, WOULD YOU LIKE TO GO NEXT?
SURE.

MY REPORT IS ON "HATCHET" BY GARY PAULSEN.
COLE

IT'S ABOUT A 13 YEAR OLD BOY...

WITH DIVORCED PARENTS...

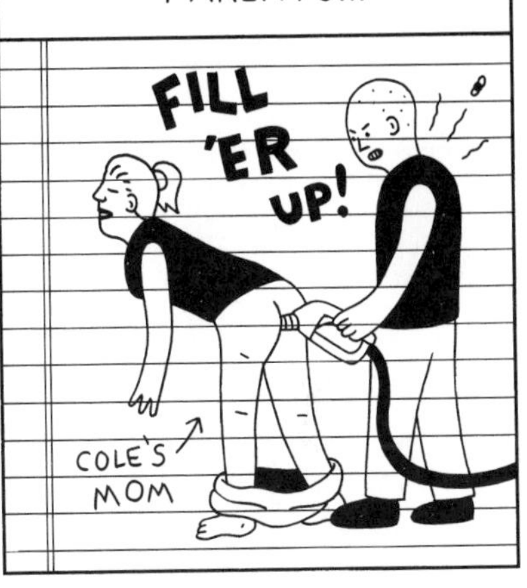

...WHOSE PLANE CRASHES IN THE WILDERNESS.

HE'S THE ONLY ONE LEFT ALIVE...

AND HE ONLY HAS A HATCHET...

CRUMPLE

BALD KNOBBE
VIGILANTES OF THE OZA

...AND HE HAS TO LEARN HOW TO SURVIVE.

KINNEY MIDDLE SCHOOL

WELCOME
BACK
STUDENTS

THE END

ROBERT SERGEL (B.1982) IS THE AUTHOR OF THE COMIC SERIES **ESCHEW,** WHICH HAS BEEN NOMINATED FOR AN IGNATZ AWARD, FEATURED IN THE BEST AMERICAN COMICS ANTHOLOGY AND WAS RELEASED AS THE COLLECTION **SPACE** BY SECRET ACRES IN 2016. HE CURRENTLY LIVES IN CAMBRIDGE, MASS.

FOR MORE INFO ON THE BALD KNOBBERS, CHECK OUT:

BALD KNOBBERS: VIGILANTES OF THE OZARKS FRONTIER
BY MARY HARTMAN AND ELMO INGENTHRON

BALD KNOBBERS: CHRONICLES OF VIGILANTE JUSTICE
BY VINCENT S. ANDERSON